Machine Learn

Python

*Programming Languages
Project*

Table of Contents8

Introduction

Congratulations on purchasing *Python Machine Learning* and thank you for doing so.

The next step is to take some time and explore more about what Python machine learning is able to do for you. These two topics are very powerful on their own, but when we are able to combine them both together, we will find that it provides us with a lot of benefits and can make it possible to work on any of the projects for making our machines and our systems smarter and stronger than ever before.

We started out this guidebook by taking a look at some of the basics that we need to know when it comes to the world of machine learning. There are a lot of benefits that come to us through machine learning and it is always a good idea to learn how this works, what the different types of machine learning are all about, and even some of the benefits and reasons to work with machine learning and other similar topics.

When we have a better understanding of how machine learning works it is time for us to move on to the second part of the equation, the idea of the Python coding language. When it comes to the best coding language to work with that helps beginners do their work and can ensure that we have enough power to handle the programming that we want to do, nothing is better than the Python coding language. We will take a look at some of the basics of coding in this language, and how you can get started with it for your own needs.

With that in mind, it is time to move on to some of the different coding libraries that you can use along with Python to complete your machine learning project. There are a ton of these libraries, and we took a look at two of the most popular data science and machine learning libraries including Scikit-Learn and TensorFlow that will help us to get that work done and see our machines become smart machines.

Once we have a good idea of how the Python language works, and some of the best machine learning libraries to use with Python, we will then explore some of the things that you can do with machine learning, and some of the best algorithms that will get the work done for you. We will look at the K-Means clustering, neural networks, Naïve Bayes, regression algorithms, and more. This can help you to take on any machine learning project with the help of Python that you want to handle.

There is so much that we are able to do with the help of Python machine learning. And this guidebook is going to take some time to look through all of the different parts so that you can create the project that you want, and sort through all of that data in no time. When you are ready to learn more about Python machine learning make sure to check out this guidebook to get you started!

There are plenty of books on this subject on the market, thanks again for choosing this one! Every effort was made to ensure it is full of as much useful information as possible, please enjoy!

Chapter 1: What is Machine Learning?

Many companies spend their time collecting a lot of data. They know that having this data on hand is going to make a big difference in how much they know about their industry, how much they know about the competition, and how much they know about their own customers. All of this provides them with a unique advantage over the competition and could be just what they need to get ahead of the game.

But collecting all of that data is not going to be the only step that needs to happen in this process. You can hold onto all of the data in the world. But if you don't know how to use that data, and you don't understand what insights and predictions are inside of that data, then it is pretty much worthless for you to use, and you may as well just throw it all away.

The trick here is that we need to be able to gather the data, and then find an effective and fast method that can search through the data, and learn something new. If you take too long to go through the data it will be outdated and have no meaning, and it wasn't worth your time either. And you need to be able to go through it and find the right insights and predictions that will actually be able to help you out.

It is possible to have someone in your company go through the information, but only if the set of data is small and easy to read through. For the larger data sets that most companies have been collecting for some time, this is not going to be an efficient way to get the work done. Despite their best intentions, there will just be too much information to sort through and look through, and they will quickly fall behind and probably make the wrong predictions.

And this is where the process of machine learning is going to come into play. With this idea, we are looking at picking out the right models and the right algorithms and use those to train a machine or a system to take care of that data. With the right algorithm in place, we can sort through a ton of data in real-time, making it easier to get the predictions that we need in no time at all. Plus, we can add in machine learning to some of the projects that we are trying to create, such as facial and voice recognition, in order to make these devices work the way that we want.

Machine learning is going to be one of the applications of artificial intelligence that can provide a system with the ability to learn, all on its own, without the help of a programmer telling the system what to do. The system can even take this a bit further and can work to improve based on its own experience, and none of this is done with the system being explicitly programmed in the process. The idea of machine learning is going to be done with a focus on the development of programs on the computer that is able to access any data you have and can then use that presented data to learn something new, and how you would like it to behave.

There are going to be a few different applications that we can look at when it comes to using machine learning. As we start to explore more about what machine learning is able to do, you may notice that over the years, it has been able to change and develop into something that programmers are going to enjoy working with more than ever. When you want to make your machine or system do a lot of the work on its own, without you having to step in and program every step, then machine learning is the right option for you.

When it comes to the world of technology, we will find that machine learning is pretty unique and can add to a level of fun to the coding that we do. There are already a lot of companies, in a variety of industries (which we will talk about in a bit), that will use machine learning and are already receiving a ton of benefits from it.

While there are already a ton of applications that we can do with the help of machine learning, some of the best methods that we can spend our time on, and that is often seen as the best to use will include:

- Statistical research: machine learning is a big part of IT now. You will find that machine learning will help you to go through a lot of complexity when looking through large data patterns. Some of the options that will use statistical research include search engines, credit cards, and filtering spam messages.
- Big data analysis: many companies need to be able to get through a lot of data in a short amount of time. They use this data to recognize how their customers spend money and even to make decisions and predictions about the future. This

used to take a long time to have someone sit through and look at the data, but now machine learning can do the process faster and much more efficiently. Options like election campaigns, medical fields, and retail stores have used machine learning for this purpose.

- Finances: some finance companies have also used machine learning. Online Stock trading has seen a rise in the use of machine learning to help make efficient and safe decisions and so much more.

As we mentioned before, these are just the start of the list of the methods you can use with machine learning, and there are countless ways that your business can use this technology. As you start to add some machine learning to your business, and you put a bit of IT to it as well, you will find that the options of what we can do with machine learning are unlimited.

While we are here, we need to take a quick look at artificial intelligence and what all of this is about. For someone who is brand new to working with machine learning and the world of technology this term, and artificial intelligence may seem a bit like it is the same thing. But machine learning and artificial intelligence are completely different, and while they work well together, we do need to understand the similarities and the differences that come with using both of these terms.

This is a term that was first brought about by a computer scientist named John McCarthy in the 1950s. AI was first described as a method that you would use for manufactured devices to learn how to copy the capabilities of humans in regard to mental tasks.

However, the term has changed a bit in modern times, but you will find that the basic idea is the same. When you implement AI, you are enabling machines, such as computers, to operate and think just like the human brain can. This is a benefit that means that these AI devices are going to be more efficient at completing some tasks than the human brain.

At first glance, this may seem like AI is the same as machine learning but they are not exactly the same. Some people who don't understand how these two terms work can think that they are the same, but the way that you use them in programming is going to make a big difference.

But machine learning is going to work in a slightly different manner. Machine learning is going to be a form of artificial intelligence that works with teaching the computer how to behave so that it can sort through some of the data that you present to the machine. And this is exactly why it has been included as a subset of data science as well. And there are a bunch of different tasks that we can use to make this work for our needs.

Machine learning is a section of data science that is going to focus specifically on having the program learn from the input and the data that the user gives to it. This helps it to make predictions in the future. For example, when you use a search engine, you would put in a term that you want to search into the bar and the engine would go through all the pages that are online in order to see what is available and will match what you want to know.

The first few times that you do these search queries, it is likely that the results will have something of interest, but you may have to go down the page a bit in order to find the information that you want. But as you keep doing this, the computer will take that information and learn from it in order to provide you with choices that are better in the future. The first time, you may click on like the sixth result, but over time, you may click on the first or second result because the computer has learned what you find valuable.

With traditional programming, this is not something that your computer can do on its own. Each person is going to do searches differently and there are millions of pages to sort through. Plus, each person who is doing their searches online will have their own preferences for what they want to show up. Conventional programming is going to run into issues when you try to do this kind of task because there are just too many variables. Machine learning has the capability to make it happen though.

The Evolution of Machine Learning

The next thing that we need to take some time to look at is the evolution of how machine learning has gone from its beginning to where it is right now. Thanks to some of the technologies of computing that are now available and brand new, the machine learning that we see in the present day will not be the same as it was in the past. In the beginning, machine learning was born from the idea of recognizing patterns, and the idea that we can actually train computers without them being specifically programmed to finish that task.

With this behind it, researchers that are interested in learning more about artificial intelligence, and what it can do, also wanted to see if they can make computers learn from the data that was presented to them. And the iterative part that comes with machine learning is so important in most of the projects that you do because as the models are exposed to the new data, they will be able to adapt in an independent manner.

What does this mean? Since the models of machine learning are seen as iterative, they are able to learn from the computations they did in the past, which helps them to produce reliable, and repeatable results and decisions. While machine learning is not something that is new but one that has gained some more momentum and is able to do so many tasks.

While it is true that these algorithms form machine learning have really been around for many years now, the ability for them to apply some of the more complex mathematical calculations over to big data doing so over and over again at an ever-increasing rate, is something that is a more recent development. And the world has been able to take ahold of this kind of technology and we are already seeing quite a few examples of how this is going to work. Some of the widely publicized examples that we can see with applications of machine learning that you may already know about include:

1. The self-driving car from Google is a good example of what machine learning can do.
2. Any online recommendations that you see, whether it is from a site like Netflix or Amazon or another website that you spent some time searching on.
3. When a business would like to know more about what their customers are saying about them on social media sites like Twitter. Machine learning can handle this by combining together with a process that is known as the linguistic rule creation.
4. Detecting fraud in the various financial worlds. This is one of the most important and more obvious uses of the technology behind machine learning.

While we are here, we need to take a moment to talk about artificial intelligence and why it is so important. Artificial intelligence is basically the broad science of being able to mimic the abilities of humans. Machine learning is going to be a subset of artificial intelligence or a type of artificial intelligence that we are able to work with.

With machine learning, we are actually able to go through the process of teaching the machine how we would like to learn. Machine learning is going to include all of the algorithms and models that a programmer needs in order to get a system to analyze the data that we have and see some good results. Without machine learning, we could hold onto the data that we collected forever, and never learn anything from it in the process.

Why Is Machine Learning So Important?

The next thing that we need to explore when it comes to machine learning is why it is so important to learn more about this type of technology. The resurgence in interest with machine learning has a lot of the same factors behind it as data mining and some of the other parts of data science that are growing as well. In fact, while machine learning has been a topic that has been around for some time, it is becoming more popular now than ever. When we add in some things like the amount of data that is available for companies to use, and the variety of information and data that we can pick from, the idea that the computational process is more powerful and less expensive, and the idea of data storage that is more affordable, we can see why machine learning has really taken off and become so popular.

Thanks to all of the factors that we have just been able to talk about previously, it has become even easier for us to quickly and automatically produce the models that we need. These models will help us to analyze bigger and more complex data, while also delivering results that are done faster, and are more accurate, than ever before. And this can all be done on a larger scale than we could imagine in the past.

And when we are able to build up these models that are more precise the organization has a better chance of really getting more advantages. For example, the company who is using these models will have a better chance of avoiding risks that they don't know about (there are always unknown risks in the business world, but learning how to avoid them can really save your business), while also identifying some of the opportunities out there that are the most profitable.

With this in mind, there are going to be a few things that we need to have in place to help us create a system of machine learning that is good and will work the way that we would like to use. Some of the things that are required for this will include data preparation capabilities, a combination of algorithms that can be advanced and basic, modeling for ensembles, the ability to scale up to large products, and processes that re automatic and iterative as well.

Who Is Using Machine Learning?

As we go through this guidebook, you will find that there are many industries, and many companies within each of these industries, who will use machine learning for their own benefits. Most industries that are already working with huge amounts of data have been able to recognize the value of using the technology of machine learning. They see that by gleaning the insights and predictions that are found inside the data, and this is often done in real-time, organizations are able to work more efficiently or gain a big advantage over the competition.

Because of the value of collecting all of this data, and all of the great benefits that come with machine learning, almost any of the companies out there that collect a lot of data will be see an improvement when they start to use machine learning. But some examples of the industries that are already benefiting from this machine learning will be:

Financial services and institutions. This will include credit unions banks, credit cards, and other companies that deal with a large number of transactions on a regular basis. These companies are going to rely on the technology that is available with machine learning for two main reasons. They use it to help find some of the best insights that are in the data so they can serve their customers better, and they use it to prevent fraud.

The insights that we find inside this data can be just as valuable as anything else. It helps provide the best investment opportunities so that investors know when they should trade. It helps the bank know what products and services to offer to their customers. And it can make sure that things like fraud are not going to happen, saving the company millions of dollars each year.

The next industry that we are going to take a look at is the government. Government agencies, including utilities and some public safety, can really use the technology that comes with machine learning because they are working with many sources of data that they are hoping to mine to get some more insights. For example, analyzing sensor data identifies ways to help us increase the amount of efficiency that we have in the process, and even save money. These industries are able to use machine learning to help them detect fraud and then minimize things like identity theft.

The world of transportation has seen a big change in the amount of machine learning that it is able to use. This industry is able to analyze the data that is collected to find the best patterns and trends, which will help the transportation industry when it is time to make more efficient routes and even with helping to predict potential problems to increase the amount of profitability that we can find in the process.

A few of the key components that come with machine learning, especially the modeling aspects and the data analysis, are going to be so important because they are the tools to delivery companies, public transportation, and other organizations of transportation and can help this industry really start to thrive.

While it may not seem like it, the world of retail can really benefit from using machine learning. Think about all of the data that retail companies are able to collect on their customers. They will collect information on what products are purchased, where the customer comes from, and even some of the demographic information on their customers as well. This information can be used to help the company to see a lot of ways that they can improve the customer service they offer, how to make more money with product recommendations, and what products they should offer next.

One example that we are able to see when it comes to working with machine learning in the retail industry is recommendation options on a website. These are based on the purchases that the customer has made. The model of machine learning is going to analyze the buying history of the customers in order to make good predictions on the items that the individual is likely to purchase next, in the hopes of getting another sale.

Many retail companies are going to rely on machine learning in order to capture the data, analyze it, and then use it to help make the shopping experience for the customer a bit more personalized. It can also be used to help find out more insights of the customer, can help with merchandise supply planning, price optimization, and making sure that the marketing department comes up with the right campaign to reach the customers.

Almost every part of the health care industry will be able to benefit from the use of machine learning. This is so great because of how it can handle some of the shortages in workers that are expected in this industry in the coming years. There are even wearable devices out there that are able to use sensors to see how the patient is doing, in real-time.

So far, the medical profession can see this help them with assistants who can direct patients to the right area with just a few questions answered, sensors that can monitor how the patient is doing, and then alerts another nurse if something is wrong (this is going to help out quite a bit with a nursing shortage, ensuring that patients who need more help receive it, but taking some of the workloads from the nurses), and can even help doctors to diagnose a patient in a fast and efficient manner.

The Basics of How Machine Learning Works

To help us get the most value out of the process of machine learning we have to make sure we pair the best algorithms with the right processes and tools. If you sort through the data with the wrong algorithms, you will end up with a mess, and will not be happy with the results and the insights that you get. Working with the right algorithms will make a big difference.

The neat thing here is that there are a ton of algorithms that you can choose from that work with machine learning. Each of these works in a slightly different manner, based on what actions you want your model to take on. Some of the examples of machine learning algorithms that we can work with include neural networks, decision trees, random forests, support vector machines, Nearest Neighbors mapping, and more.

There are also a number of tools and processes that we are able to rely on to help handle all of the different parts of your model. As we already know at this point, it is not going to be just about all of the algorithms, even though they are important. Ultimately, the secret to getting the most value out of all that big data you have been collecting is going to lie in pairing together the best algorithms for the task that you are working with. Some of the tools and processes that you can use along with the right algorithm will include:

1. Comprehensive management and data quality.
2. Automated ensemble evaluation of the model to help see where the best performers will show up.

3. GUIs for helping to build up the models that you want along with the process flows being built up as well.
4. Easy deployment of this so that you can get results that are reliable and repeatable in a quick manner.
5. Interactive exploration of the data and even some visualizations that help us to view the information easier.
6. A platform that is integrated and end to end to help with the automation of some of the data to decision process that you would like to follow.
7. A tool to compare the different models of machine learning to help us identify the best one to use in a quick and efficient manner.

As we can see in this chapter, there is so much that we can do with machine learning. Machine learning is one of the best ways to handle some of the data science that we want to complete, helping to move our company into the future, and beat out the competition. There are a lot of industries who are already jumping on board with the use of machine learning, and there are already so many who are looking to add it in as well.

And that is the neat thing with machine learning. It can be adapted and changed to work with a ton of different companies, and on many different processes, based on the specific needs of that company. Finding the right algorithm, or even the right suite of algorithms, to get the work done can be one of the best options to help us provide better customer service, pick out the best products to offer to our customers, and so much more.

Chapter 2: The Different Types of Machine Learning?

Now that we know a bit more about machine learning and how it can be used, it is time for us to take things a step further and look more into the different types of machine learning. While each of the algorithms that we use will be slightly different from one another, we can remember that they can all fit into one of three general areas with each other to give you the results that you are looking for. We will see that when it comes to machine learning, we can work with supervised machine learning, unsupervised machine learning, and reinforcement machine learning. Let's take a look at each of these and see how we are able to use them for our benefits when working with Python machine learning at the same time.

Supervised Machine Learning

The first type of machine learning algorithm that we will take a look at is known as supervised machine learning. This machine learning type is the kind where someone is going to train the system, and the way that they do this is by making sure to provide input, with the corresponding output, to the system so it knows the right answers. You also have to take the time to furnish the feedback into the system based on whether the system or the machine was accurate in the predictions that it made.

This is a process that takes time, and you need to have a good deal of data present in order to make it happen. The trainer has to show a bunch of different and diverse examples to that system, and then also show the system the output, or the corresponding answers, so that it can learn how it is supposed to behave in the process as well.

After the completion of the training, the algorithm will need to apply what it learned from the data earlier on to make the best predictions. The concept that comes with supervised learning can be seen to be similar to learning under the supervision of a teacher to their students. The teacher is going to give a lesson to the students with some examples, and then the student is going to derive the new rules and knowledge from these examples. They can then take the knowledge and apply it to different situations, even if they don't match up directly to the examples that the teacher gives.

When we are looking at supervised machine learning, it is also a good thing to know the difference between the classification problems and the regression problems. A regression problem is going to be when the target is a numeric value of some kind. But the classification is going to be a class or a tag. A regression task can help to determine the average cost of all the homes in a town, while the classification would help to determine what type of flower is in the picture based on the length of their petals.

Supervised learning is going to occur when you pick out an algorithm that is able to learn the right response to the data a user input to it. There are several ways that supervised machine learning can do this. It can look at examples and other targeted responses that you provide to the computer. You could include values or strings of labels to help the program learn the right way to behave.

When it comes to supervised machine learning, you will find that it is a simple process, though it does take some time because you have to go through and actually teach the computer or the machine how to behave in a manual manner. One example of how this can work though is when a teacher is in a classroom and they want to start teaching the students a new topic.

One of the methods that they are able to use to make this happen is to grab some examples of a situation or a lesson, and then show these to the class. The students, by listening and studying, will start to learn and even memorize these examples because they know that the information the teacher is providing will give them the general rules that they need on the topic.

Over time, and with more practice on this, the students are going to understand the topic better and can use it to answer those questions the proper way, and even make good predictions on how they should do things in the future. Later on, when the students are given these exact examples and even ones that are similar, they have a good idea of how to respond. And then if there is another example that comes up that doesn't match with what you learned, you still know how to respond as well.

Unsupervised Machine Learning

The second type of machine learning that we need to take a look at is known as unsupervised learning. This can help us out with machine learning quite a bit, but we have to see that it is quite different compared to how we work with the supervised machine but it is going to help us to really do something new with the coding that we have.

You will find that with unsupervised machine learning, you are not going to provide the system with the output data to teach it how to behave. This is because the goal with the machine is to learn what it is saying based on the unknown input that the person is going to use with it on their own rather than having the programmer do all of the work. This is an approach that is known as deep learning (we will explore this a further on in one of the next chapters), and it is going to be more of an iterative approach that can review all of the data at hand and then figure out the right conclusions to make.

What this does is make an unsupervised learning approach more suitable for use in a variety of processing tasks, which can be more complex than what you would do with supervised learning algorithms. This means that the learning algorithms that are unsupervised are going to learn just from examples, without getting any responses to it. The algorithm will strive to find the patterns that come from those examples all on its own, rather than being told the answers.

Many of the recommender types of systems that you encounter, such as when you are purchasing something online, are going to work with the help of an unsupervised learning algorithm. In this case the algorithm is going to derive what to suggest to you to purchase based on what you went through and purchased before. The algorithm then has to estimate the customers you resemble the most based on your purchases and then will provide you with some good recommendations from there.

As we mentioned previously, there is more than one type of machine learning that you can work with.

Supervised learning is the first one. It is designed for you to show examples to the computer and then you teach it how to respond based on the examples that you presented. There are a lot of programs where this kind of technique is going to work well, but the idea of showing thousands of examples to your computer can seem tedious. Plus, there are many programs where this is not going to work all that well.

It is at this point where we are going to start seeing some of the algorithms of unsupervised machine learning come into play. And that is why we need to take some more time to really explore some of the additional tasks that this kind of learning, and the algorithms that go with it, are able to learn about in the whole process.

Unsupervised learning is going to be one of the methods that will show up when the algorithm is able to make a mistake and then learn from it. And the machine is able to do all of this without any kind of associated response showing up and telling it how to behave. What this means is that when you use an algorithm that fits into this category, the machine is going to be in charge of figuring out and then analyzing the patterns in the data based on the kind of input that you hand over to it.

Now, you can imagine that we are able to see a variety of algorithm types that will fit under the category of unsupervised machine learning. No matter which type of algorithm you want to work with, it is able to take that kind of data, and then will restructure it in a manner where all of the data can fall into a class. This is a great thing for you to see happen because when it comes to the coding you do, it will make it easier to look over it at a later stage when you are ready.

There are a lot of projects that will rely on unsupervised learning. This is because while it takes a bit of time for the computer to learn on its own, it doesn't take up as much time for the programmer to get things up and running. The programmer doesn't have to be there handling it all, and we know that the machine with unsupervised learning it is successful with the work that it's doing, it can get through a lot of the different processes and tasks that would take a long time to complete if someone manually did them.

Adding in the Reinforcement Learning

And finally, we are going to take some time exploring the third type of machine learning, known as reinforcement learning. This is a new type of machine learning that will happen and work anytime the algorithm is

Presented with some examples that aren't labeled ahead of time. This is often seen as similar to what happens with unsupervised learning and for those who are not familiar with machine learning, the two categories of learning may seem like the same.

However, this one is going to work more on a trial and error method with some positive and negative feedback , based on the solution that is proposed by the algorithm, and whether it matches up to what the programmer was looking for. This one is often going to be used when we want to work with an application where the algorithm has to make some decisions, and then these decisions are going to come with a consequence based on what the decision is all about.

Errors are fine in this because they are going to become useful in the learning process when they are associated with a penalty such as loss of time, cost, and pain. In the process of reinforced learning, some actions are going to be more likely to succeed while others are less likely to succeed.

Machine learning processes are going to be similar to what we see with predictive modeling and data mining. In both cases, patterns are then going to be adjusted inside the program accordingly. A good example of machine learning is the recommender system. If you purchase an item online, you will then see an ad that is going to be related to that item.

There are some people who see reinforcement learning as the same thing as unsupervised learning because they are so similar, but it is important to understand that they are different. First, the input that is given to these algorithms will need to have some mechanisms for feedback. You can set these up to be either negative or positive based on the algorithm that you decide to write out.

So, if you decide to work with this method, you are going to work with a machine learning technique that is similar to trial and error. Think about when you are doing something with a child when they go through and perform an action that you don't want them to repeat, you will stop by letting them know the action is not something they are allowed to do. You explain that they need to stop, or they will end up in a time out or another action that you want here.

With this in mind, if the child does that action again, then they get the consequences that you set. But, you can do this with positive reinforcement as well. If that same child comes and does something that you approve of, and something that you want them to repeat, you spend some time praising them and making sure that they know that their did a good job. This helps the child feel good, and they are more likely to repeat the same thing again. Through these steps, both the positive and the negative reinforcement, the child is starting to learn how he should behave.

As you can see, there is a lot that comes with machine learning, and each of these categories of the algorithms can help us see how there are so many tasks that we can use them with. Figuring out which kind of project we want to focus on, and which machine learning algorithm will go with that, can make a difference in the way that we can benefit from machine learning overall.

Chapter 3: The Benefits of Using Machine Learning

When it comes to using machine learning for your business, there are a lot of benefits that come with it. Many businesses are jumping on board because this is really a great way to learn something about the industry, the competition, and about the customers who help run your business in the first place. With all of the buzz that is running around big data, machine learning, and artificial intelligence, it is really important to learn about all of the benefits and applications that come with machine learning for their business.

A lot of businesses are now familiar with the term of machine learning but they may not know exactly what this is able to do for their business, or what business-related problems it is able to solve. Machine learning is a data analysis process that will leverage the machine learning algorithms (some of which we will learn about in this guidebook), to make sure we can learn from existing data and can help our systems and machines find all of the hidden insights, without someone having to program it all.

With Microsoft Azure, Amazon, and Google launching their own cloud machine learning platforms, we have a good inside look into what machine learning and artificial intelligence are able to do for us. What is surprising though is that all of us have witnessed this machine learning without actually being aware of it. For example, if you have ever used an email account, Spam detection is going to be an example of machine learning. If you have seen some of the Face tagging through Facebook, then you have worked with machine learning as well.

As we can see here, there are a lot of times when we will see machine learning helping out the world around you, and many businesses are going to join and see what it can do for us. But first, we need to be able to explore more about some of the benefits that come with machine learning, and why it is such a popular method to work with. Some of the top business benefits that we can see when we work to implement machine learning will include:

Can Make Product Marketing Easier

The first benefit that we can see with machine learning is that it is going to help an enterprise find more than one method to promote their products, and they have a better way to make accurate forecasts on sales. Machine learning is going to offer a huge advantage to the marketing and the sales sectors and some of these include:

It can help us consume a lot of data from an unlimited number of sources. Machine learning virtually consumes an unlimited amount of data. The consumed data can then be used in order to review and make the needed modifications to the sales and marketing strategies usually based on some of the behavioral patterns that we see in the customer. Once the business has been able to train their model, they will be able to identify the variables that are the most relevant. In addition, you will be able to get focused feeds of data by foregoing long and complicated integrations at the same time.

The next thing that we need to focus on is that machine learning can help us to do a fast analysis prediction and processing. The rate at which machine learning is going to consume data and identify relevant data makes it possible for a business to take the right actions at the right time. For example, it is going to optimize the best offer for your customers. Because of this, the customer is going to see the right offer at a given point of time, without the business having to invest the time to plan and make the right ad visible to your customers at the right time.

And finally, we can use this to help us interpret past customer behaviors. Machine learning is great for helping you analyze the data that is related to past behaviors or outcomes and then interpret it. Therefore, based on the new and unique way that you will be able to make better predictions of customers behaviors.

Can Facilitate Accurate Medical Predictions

In the healthcare industry, machine learning is able to help out so much. This industry is able to help us with identifying patients who are high risk, can make diagnoses that are nearly perfect, will recommend some of the best medications for the particular disease or disorder and can predict the rate of readmission of that patient.

These are going to be based on the available sets of data of anonymous patient records as well as the symptoms that are then exhibited. Better recommendations about medication and almost accurate diagnoses can help us to facilitate faster patient recovery without the need for tests and medication that are not necessary. This helps to keep the medical costs down to a minimum and will improve patient health at the same time.

Simplifies Documentation with Data Entry

There are times when we need to get the information entered into our database in a quick and efficient manner. If there is a lot of data to sort through, and not a lot of time to get it done, it may seem like an impossible task. But with the help of machine learning, you can get the time-sensitive document of the data entry that you need to focus on.

Data duplication and some inaccuracies that can show up are going to be big issues that organizations are going to face when they want to automate the process of data entry. Well, this situation can be improved quite a bit by improved by predictive modeling and machine learning algorithms. This means that when you utilize some of this you will be able to use machine learning to make your system perform time-intensive data entry tasks, leaving your more skilled resources free to focus on other duties that add more value to your business.

Improves Precision Financial Rules

Another benefit that we will be able to see when it comes to using machine learning is that it really helps out the finance sector. Some of the common benefits that we will see in the financial world, though not all of them, can include things like detecting fraud, loan underwriting algorithmic trading, and portfolio management.

In addition to this, according to one report called "The Future of Underwriting," machine learning is already making a big impact because it can continually assess the data you have, and then analyze and detect a lot of the nuances and the anomalies that show up in that information, even if these would be hard for a person to do on their own. This is going to help out when it is time to improve the precision of any financial models and rules that we work with.

Can Help with Spam Detection

No one wants to get onto an email server and have their inbox fill up with spam and other emails that have nothing to do with them. This can be boring, and sometimes frustrating. There is so much spam that comes into emails all of the time, and when it starts to interfere with the usual use that you have with your inbox, this can make it hard to get back to others, see important information, and more.

Spam detection was actually one of the first problems that machine learning was able to help out with. Just a few years ago, email providers would use some of the techniques of machine learning that were rule-based to help filter out the spam, helping users get more of the emails that they want, and less of what they don't want.

With the help of machine learning, spam filters are able to make new rules with the help of their neural networks, effectively eliminating some of the spam mail that has been coming in the whole time. The neural networks, which we will explore in more detail in a bit, are able to recognize some of the bad emails and the various junk mail simply by evaluating the rules across a huge network of compilers and then preventing those from making their way into your email inbox.

Increases the Efficiency Found in Manufacturing

Another industry that is going to benefit from working with the machine learning algorithms that we will talk about in a bit is the world of manufacturing. This machine learning is going to help the company to increase its own efficiency of predictive maintenance in various parts of this industry.

In the past few years, manufacturing firms have been able to put various practices into place including corrective and preventive maintenance practices. However, while these can help the business complete a lot of different tasks it can be costly and is not the most efficient method to work with. And this is why machine learning can definitely help the company to see some results with their work in no time.

Machine learning is going to come into play and will help with the creation of highly efficient predictive maintenance plans. Following these plans will be helpful to the company because it will ensure that we can minimize how likely it is that unexpected failures are going to show up, which helps the company reduce any of the activities for preventative maintenance that are not necessary for them.

A Better Understanding of the Customer

One of the big reasons that industries all throughout the world choose to add in some machine learning is because it helps us to really know more about our customers and what they are looking for when it comes to using our product or why they choose our company over the competition. There is so much that we can learn when using machine learning on our customers, and many companies who choose to do this will find that it makes them more competitive, no matter what industry they are on.

To start with, we need to take a look at customer segmentation. This along with something known as lifetime value prediction, is seen as some of the biggest challenges that marketers are already facing today. Sales and marketing units are going to gather up an enormous amount of data that is relevant for them, from a wide variety of channels in the process. This could include sources like social media local data, website visitors, and email campaigns.

Even with all of this information from a lot of different sources, the company needs to take things a step further and figure out how they can use the information, rather than just having it sit there doing nothing. With some of the right machine learning algorithms in place it will be easier to sort through that data and find the relevant customer information to help make your business as successful as possible.

For example, you can choose to use the data you have collected in order to find out more about the behavior patterns of a specific set of users during your set trial period. This, when used properly, will help to predict the probability of conversion of your customers from that trial version over to the paid version. Such model is going to trigger the interventions of the customer in order to better engage the customers in the trial, and see if you are able to convert them early on.

Recommending the Right Products

One aspect that is really growing in popularity and becoming critical to how well the company is going to do overtime is the idea of product recommendations for the customers. This is going to be a big part of any marketing and sales strategy that the company uses including upselling and cross-selling to its customers. Machine learning is going to provide a model that can analyze the purchase history of a particular customer. Then it can identify other products that are in the inventory of products for a customer to see which ones a customer is going to be the most interested in.

The right machine learning algorithm is going to be able to find all of the hidden patterns in your data and then will group them so that similar products are into clusters. This is going to be a form of unsupervised learning, which is one of the machine learning algorithms that we talked about before that is able to get the machine or the system to learn on its own.

This kind of model can be so good for your business. When it is set up the right way, it is going to help a business make the best product recommendations to their customers each time, which is going to make it more likely that the customer will purchase additional products. And the more products that a customer is willing to purchase, the more that it helps the business to grow and earn more profits. In this manner, we can see that unsupervised machine learning is going to help us out in creating a superior product-based recommendation system out there.

All of these applications show us exactly how machine learning is going to make a difference when it comes to helping us grow our business, no matter what industry we are in at the time. This type of technology is able to help out with a lot of different things, including cross-selling and upselling, making it so much easier to work with overall.

There is a lot of good that this machine learning algorithm is able to work with.

As you can see here, there are a lot of benefits out there when it comes to using machine learning. For example it is going to be a great way for businesses to handle the different challenges that come with them and can ensure that we will see some great improvements against the competition. From learning what customers want to figure out how to cut out waste, give a better diagnosis of your patients, and more, you will find that machine learning is going to provide you with everything that your business needs to really improve and beat out the competition.

Chapter 4: A Quick Look at Deep Learning

The next topic that we need to take a look at is the idea of deep learning. This type of learning can help us get a lot of our projects done when we are working with the algorithms and machine learning that we will take a look at as we go through this guidebook. So, let's take a look at what deep learning is all about, and how we will be able to use it for our own business to see a lot of improvements along the way.

What is Deep Learning All About?

The first thing we need to take a look at here is what deep learning is all about. To keep this simple, deep learning is going to be a function that we see with artificial intelligence. This deep learning is able to imitate the working of the human brain but it puts it into a system or a machine of our choice. This works by being able to process the data and then create a pattern for use in decision making that is based on data, rather than on a hunch. This helps the company produce better results for their customers, beat out the competition, release some of the best products on the market, and ensure that they can reduce costs and see more results.

Deep learning is actually going to be a subset that we can look at when it comes to the world of artificial intelligence and machine learning. And it takes things a bit further because it has a network of capable learning unsupervised from data that doesn't come with any labels, or is a bit unstructured. This type of learning is also going to be known as deep neural networks or deep neural learning based on how you will use it.

How to Get Deep Learning to Work

Deep learning is a process that has really evolved quite a bit with the advent and the growth of the digital era, which has helped to bring about a big explosion of data in all forms that we could ever imagine and from every region of the world. It is amazing how much data businesses are able to collect overall, and as soon as they are able to figure out what insights are in that data and how they are able to use it, they can really provide themselves with an easy and efficient manner to beat out the competition.

This data, which is going to go by the name of big data, is drawn from a large variety of sources, including online, social media, e-commerce platforms, online cinemas. Each business will have to determine where they would like to gather the information, or the big data, from, based on the questions they would like to have answered in the first place.

This enormous amount of information is going to be really helpful, and it is often readily accessible and can be shared through a lot of applications, like cloud computing, so that the business is able to share it with others and find what they need at any time.

However, the data is often unstructured and hard to sort through, and many times the company will gather the data for so long that it is so vast, simply because there is just so much of it to work with. This means that if a human manually goes through and tries to sort through the information, it could take them decades to comprehend all of it and get the right information out of it all. This may have been the only way for companies to go through the information in the past, but it is not always the most efficient.

If you are gathering all of this information, you want to get the predictions and insights out of that information, you do not want to wait decades to gather that information and read the insights. This takes way too long and you will be left behind in the dust. And when you are done, there will be decades worth of new information sitting there, waiting for you to dive into at the same time. It is just not efficient for a company to work manually going through all of that data, because things will get missed, and it will take too long.

This is why a lot of companies are starting to see some of the incredible potentials that can result from taking a look through all of the wealth of the information. And they recognize the importance that comes with having a system that is able to sort through that information efficiently and quickly. This means that these same companies are going to work to adapt their artificial systems to handle the work on their own and to handle automated support.

One thing to remember here is that deep learning is able to learn from all of the huge amounts of unstructured data. This is something that could take years for humans to manually go through the whole process, but with the help of deep learning and other tasks of artificial intelligence, a machine can go through and see the information and insights inside in no time.

Machine Learning Vs. Deep Learning

Now we need to take a look at how machine learning and deep learning are going to work with one another. One of the most common techniques that we are able to use with artificial intelligence, especially when it comes to processing all of the big data, is machine learning. Remember from before that machine learning is going to be a self-adaptive algorithm that is going to teach itself how to get better with analyzing and finding patterns the more that it gains some experience or when it adds in some new data as well.

Let's take a look at how all of this can work. If there is a company that specializes in digital payments that want to look at this process to help detect the occurrence or any potential there is of fraud in their system, it would maybe take some of the tools for machine learning to help them with this purpose in particular. The computational algorithm that we are able to build into a computer model will be able to take a look at, and process, all of the transactions that happen on the digital platform, and then can find some patterns in the set of data, while pointing out to someone, usually the person in charge of fraud detection, when it finds some kind of anomaly in the pattern.

Deep learning, which is going to be a subset of machine learning, is going to come into role because it is able to utilize some of the hierarchical levels of various artificial neural networks. This is done in order to help carry out some of the new and more advanced processes that come with machine learning. These artificial neural networks are going to be set up like the human brain, with the neuron nodes connecting to one another with the help of a structure that appears to be a web.

While some of the traditional programs that you can work with can build up an analysis with the data in a manner that is more linear many programmers prefer to work with the hierarchal function. This is because this kind of function of deep learning is able to make a machine process data, even with the nonlinear approach.

In the past, one of the traditional approaches to detecting things like money laundering or fraud, the customers would rely on the amount of transaction that ensued. This means that only the really large transactions would be the ones that are caught at all, and the only ones that would rise up a big red flag.

Of course, these are not the only transactions that could be bad. And sometimes it is possible that someone trying to commit fraud would do a bunch of small transactions quickly rather than working with large transactions. When this happens, the person could get away with a lot of different transactions in a small amount of time, but it would not be found because the transaction amount, for the individual transaction was small enough that the system would not catch it. And this ends up costing the financial institution a lot of money over the years with fraudulent charges.

The neat thing with machine learning, and working on a nonlinear method of deep learning, we can look at more than just the amount of money when we are trying to detect fraud. For example, the algorithm may be set up to look at things like the type of retailer, the IIP address, the geographic location, and the time to determine if this is a purchase or a transaction that the customer would likely be partaking in or not.

The first layer that we will see when the neural network tries to process the input of raw data like the amount of the transaction, and then will pass it on to the next layer, with this information being the output now. The second layer of the neural network is going to be able to process the information that it got from the previous layer by including some additional information like the IP address of the user and passes this on with the result. This continues until all of the layers of the neural network are done.

The next layer that is here is going to take the second layer's information, and then will include some of the raw data that you have things like the geographic location, and will make the pattern of the machine even better. This is going to continue on through the levels that come with this neuron network. The number of levels that come with the neural network will depend on what process you are trying to complete.

With this in mind, let's review and take a closer look at some of the key takeaways that come with deep learning. These will include:

1. Deep learning is going to be a function of artificial intelligence that is able to mimic the workings that we see with the human brain, particularly when it comes to processing the data. This then provides us with the information we need for decision making.
2. Deep learning with artificial intelligence is also going to help us learn from the data. This includes learning out of the data that is unlabeled and unstructured.
3. Deep learning, which is one of the subsets of machine learning can often be used to help with a variety of different situations including things like money laundering and detecting fraud.

An Example of What Happens with Deep Learning

Let's take a look at some of the things that happen with deep learning and an example of what we can expect when we add in some deep learning to the work that we want to do with all of that data. We are going to explore the fraud detection system that we talked about earlier in this chapter and see exactly how this kind of system will work with deep learning, machine learning, and artificial intelligence.

Using that detection system from before, we are going to create a machine learning system that will help us create our own model that has the parameters we want to be built around the number of dollars that a user will receive or send. With these parameters in place, it is easier to create a deep learning method that is able to build on the results that we see with machine learning in the process.

Each layer of this neural network is going to build on its previous layer with some added data, like a retailer, the social media even, credit score, sender, user, IP address, and other features. Without something like machine learning, we would see that this kind of process could take years to complete, and a manual method would not work the way that we would like.

The deep learning algorithms that we want to use here are trained to not just go through and create some patterns from all of the transactions, but these algorithms also need to know when there is a pattern involved that signals the need for an investigation, or not. The final layer with this example is going to send a message or an alert back to the analyst. And based on what the algorithm finds, and what the analyst finds as well, the account could be frozen to prevent further issues until all of the pending investigations that were already started are complete.

Deep learning is going to be used in a lot of different industries to help out with many different tasks. Commercial apps that would rely on image recognition, open-source platforms that have recommendation apps for the consumer, and even medical research tools that are able to explore the possibility of reusing drugs for some of the new ailments, are all examples of what we are going to be able to do with machine learning.

There is just so much that we are able to work with when it comes to deep learning. Think about all of the different functions and tasks that deep learning, along with artificial intelligence and machine learning will be able to help your business to do. Rather than working on all of this manually and missing out on important facts and taking too long the algorithms that come with machine learning and deep learning can step in and help you get this done fast and efficiently.

Deep learning is something that can benefit pretty much any business and this guidebook is going to take some time to explore the various parts and the different algorithms that we need. When you are ready to dive into some of the different algorithms that some with this process, you will need to have a better understanding of deep learning, along with machine learning. When these come together with the Python language, you will find that it can really help your business to thrive.

Chapter 5: Adding in Some Python with the Scikit-Learn and TensorFlow Library

Before we start to take a look at some of the different algorithms and codes that we are able to use with machine learning with the help of Python, we need to have a good idea of some of the best data science and machine learning libraries that we can rely on. These libraries are going to help expand out some of the capabilities that come with Python so that we can create these models and the algorithms that we want to use for a variety of purposes.

When it comes to focusing our energy on doing some of the tasks that we already discussed with machine learning, nothing is better to use than the Python language. There are other coding languages that can handle some of the tasks of machine learning, but none of them are going to provide the power, the capabilities, and the ease of use as we are able to find with the Python coding language. Many of the different libraries and extensions that you want to do with machine learning are going to rely on the Python language, so learning how to write some codes in this language can be a great option.

There are a ton of benefits that can come with the Python language. First, it was designed to work with beginners, with those who have never done coding in the past. This language is written in the English language, and it keeps things as simple to work through as possible which can add some ease of mind to those who are writing codes for the first time.

Even though Python is a beginner language, it still has a lot of the power and strength that you need to get the complex coding for machine learning done. It works well with a variety of libraries to ensure that all of your machine learning tasks can get done. Add in the large community of other programmers and developers who can help you out, a strong traditional library and great extensions that you can add in with this library, along with some of the other features that are available, and it is easy to see exactly why programmers will want to work with the Python library to help them with all of their machine learning tasks.

There are a lot of libraries and extensions that you can add in with Python in order to do some of the amazing tasks that come with machine learning. But the two main libraries that we are going to take a moment to learn about here will include TensorFlow and Scikit-Learn. Both of these are powerful data science and scientific libraries and will ensure that we are able to do the various algorithms that we will talk about in a bit. Let's dive right in and see how both of these libraries are going to work for us.

The Scikit-Learn Library

The first type of library that we need to spend some time on is the Scikit-Learn library. This one is going to be a bit different than some of the other options out there, but this is what makes it so useful to use for machine learning and various other data science kinds of projects. This one will also need to work with a few other Python machine learning libraries, so it is important to get a few of these on your system along with the Python files before you try to use the Scikit-Learn library.

The Scikit-Learn library is going to be helpful because it provides users with many algorithms that they can work with that are compatible with Python as well. These include algorithms for unsupervised and supervised machine learning. We will learn more about some of these algorithms as we go through the other chapters in this guidebook but you will find that many of the topics we discuss will talk about this library and how it can write out the various algorithms we need to create our own models.

Scikit-Learn has been in use mainly as one of the machine learning libraries that we use with Python. It already contains many types of algorithms that can help with clustering, classification, and regression-based on what your goals are with your project.

Some of the algorithms that are available through the Scikit-Learn library, and that we will talk about in a bit, will include gradient boosting, random forests, DBSCAN, support vector machines, and k-means algorithms. Add to this that the Scikit-Learn library was designed so that it would work well with a few of the other libraries that are out there for machine learning and data science. For example many times when we download this library, we are going to find that downloading the NumPy and the SciPy libraries to name a few can be really helpful.

The Scikit-Learn library, even on its own without some of the other options, is going to be done with the help of the Python coding language and with some of the different algorithms that are present with this library, they will also use a bit of Cython to help finish it off. This is the best way to ensure that some of the models and algorithms that you create are going to be the best and highest quality in terms of performance and more

As a programmer who is getting into machine learning and some of the neat things that we can do with it, you will quickly find that the Scikit-Learn library is one of the best options to go with for building up various machine learning models. The good news here is that the library is considered open-sourced which allows you to step in and write the codes you want, and even download the program, without having to pay or worry about the development of the library at all.

TensorFlow Library

The second library that we need to explore is the TensorFlow library and how it can help us handle a lot of the different tasks that we want to do with machine learning. This is more of a framework that we can bring out to handle the various algorithms. Often programmers are going to like this framework because it provides them with some help when they do models for deep learning. It can also work for a few other tasks in the process as well.

The library of TensorFlow is going to be useful because it handles lots of graphs of data flow and is really good at using these graphs for some of the numerical computations. Compared to some of the other methods that you can use with this process, and even some of the other libraries, machine learning is made easier when we add in TensorFlow.

There are a number of tasks that TensorFlow is able to help out with machine learning. Some of the tasks that TensorFlow is especially good with is helping us to acquire or gather up any data that we want to use and can help us to use machine learning to properly train the various models that you want to use. We can use this process to help make predictions of the information that we have, and it even comes with the tools that are needed to modify some of the future results that we see. Since all of these are very critical parts that we can do with machine learning, we can see why it is such a good idea to work with TensorFlow and machine learning.

Let's take a look at some of the histories that comes behind this library. This is one of the libraries that was developed thanks to the Google Brain Team. This group used this library to help them take some of the tasks of machine learning and scale it up to some really large projects. TensorFlow is going to help us bring together the algorithms for deep learning with the algorithms of machine learning and then it will make these more useful with a metaphor in common in the process.

TensorFlow is going to be one of the libraries that rely on Python, so if you have learned how to work with this library, this is going to make things easier. The front end of all of this will be reliant on Python and most of the coding you will want to do when developing machine learning and deep learning algorithms will be done in Python. When you execute the codes though, the language is going to switch around a bit, and you will find all of your work is executed with high-performance C++.

Your overall goals with the data you are working with, or with the model you would like to create, will determine what we are able to do when it comes to using the TensorFlow library. This library, in particular, is very helpful when it comes to building, training, and running some deep neural networks. And some of the tasks that can happen because of all this are going to include image recognition natural language processing, recurrent neural networks, and even word embedding.

As you can see, there is a lot to love when it comes to both of these coding libraries. They both work with the Python language, and they are both going to help with some even more complicated processes that come with machine learning and deep learning as well. Installing them is free to do and only takes a few minutes and they will sync up to your Python system as well. There are many tasks that we are able to add to this process, and learning how to use them with the help of the TensorFlow and the Scikit-Learn library can make creating models and algorithms with the help of Python so much easier.

Chapter 6: Other Python Libraries That Work Well with Machine Learning

While we took some time to look at a few of the best libraries that work with machine learning and Python, there are definitely quite a few more that we can bring into the mix to help you complete some of the tasks that you would like to get done within this field of study. Some of the other Python machine learning libraries that we can consider looking at and exploring will include:

1. **NumPy:** This is a great option to work with when you have a more scientific task to complete with the help of the Python language. This library stands for Numerical Python and it is going to provide us with a bunch of features that are useful for operating on a matrix or an n-array if you need it. This one can help us with some of the mathematical operations that we need to handle as well.

2. **SciPy:** This is the second library that we are going to take a look at and it works well when we want to do processes that involve science and engineering. SciPy is going to contain some of the modules for things like statistics, integration,

75

optimization, and linear algebra. The main functionality that we get with this library is going to build on NumPy, and the arrays can make a lot of use of NumPy. It is going to provide us with efficient numerical routines as optimization and numerical integrations in the process.

3. **Pandas:** The Pandas library is another important one that we are able to work with. Pandas are going to be a Python package that is designed to do work with data that is relational and labeled, and the data is going to be more intuitive and simpler. Pandas are going to be one of the best libraries to work with to handle some of the work that we need to do with data wrangling. It is designed for quick and easy data manipulation aggregation, and visualization as well.

4. **Matplotlib**: This is a great option to work with if you need to complete some kind of visualization when we work with the data we have. This is going to be a great software that can help Python do well with some of the graphs and other sources of visualization that you would like to create. With a bit of effort in this library, you are able to create almost any kind of visualization that you would like. Some of the options that you can go with will include:

   a. Line plot
   b. Spectrograms
   c. Quiver plots
   d. Stem plots
   e. The contour plots

f. Pie charts

g. Histograms and bar charts

h. Scatter plots.

5. **Theano:** This is another great machine learning library that we are able to work with because it can bring in some help with multi-dimensional arrays similar to what we see with NumPy, but we will take a look at the math operations and expressions. The important thing for us to understand here though is that it is able to implement with NumPy on some of the lower-level operations that are present in it. It also optimizes the use of CPU and GPU, making the performance of the data-intensive computation faster than other libraries can do.

6. **Keras:** And finally, we need to take a look at the library that is known as Keras. This one is going to be a library that is open-sourced and is used to help build up some high-level neural networks in the process as well. It is able to stay minimalistic in the process, with a high level of extensibility to it. It also has backends of Theano and TensorFlow that work with it to add in some extra power. This is an easy coding library to work with and it will keep going with some quick prototyping.

There are a lot of great libraries out there that are able to help you work more with machine learning and the Python language at the same time. Being able to combine them together and use them at the right time is going to make a big difference in the results that you are able to see in the process. Try a few of these out and see how they are able to help you get started with some of your own machine learning processes at the same time.

Chapter 7: Creating Your Own Neural Networks

The first kind of algorithm that we are going to take a look at is going to be the neural network. This is a complicated topic in some cases but you will find that it is going to allow you a lot of different opportunities with the machines and the systems that we are able to work with. These will fit under the example of an unsupervised machine learning algorithm. We will see that these networks are going to be used with machine learning can be used a lot because they will help you to take a look through a lot of data and see what insights and patterns are inside there. There are many different levels that are going to happen here, but it is going to be more effective, and often a lot faster than what a human would be able to do.

When we work with the neural network, we will see that each of the different layers that the system goes through will spend a bit of time checking to see if there is a pattern there, such as a pattern in an image. If the system is able to see that there is a pattern when it comes to the next layer, it is then going to start setting itself up to move to the next layer. This process will continue on and one, with one layer after another, until the neural network is out of layers and it has created an algorithm that we can work with.

We are going to focus mainly on how the neural network is going to work when it comes to creating image recognition and the way that the system will go through all of the various layers to figure out what is in the image. There are a lot of other methods we can use though in order to see the amazing tactics and techniques that come with neural networks so keep these in mind.

When the image has been looked over and the algorithm can come back with a good prediction of what is inside the image (this is going to happen when the algorithm has stopped seeing a new pattern in the image), there are going to be a few different actions that we are able to see based on how we set up the program to work.

If the algorithm was able to make its way through the process that we talked about above, and it saw some success at sorting through all of the layers, it is going to be prepared to make a prediction about what is found inside. If the machine is correct with the prediction it makes then the neurons of this system will strengthen. The more times the algorithm is right, the stronger these neurons will become.

The reason that this method is going to work is that it is run by artificial intelligence. AI is able to help create the strong associations that occur between the object and the patterns. The more times that the system sees all of these images and make the right predictions the more efficient the system becomes when you turn it on and use it again and again.

Now, this may seem like we are giving the algorithm too much credit for some of the things that we are giving to it. But when we examine how these neural networks work a bit closer, we will find that it works in a way that is similar to how the human mind works and how the neurons are going to become our best friend with a lot of the machine learning work that we would like to accomplish.

Let's take a look at how this works. Let's say that we have a goal for a project where we would like to create a program that can take a picture that you add to it, and then, after going through all of the steps and the layers that the neural network needs to do, it is able to provide you with a prediction on what image is found inside of that image.

If you have gone through and set up the neural network in the proper manner, then it is going to be able to look at that image and make a prediction that is correct. Maybe the image that is presented is of a car, when the neural network is working properly, it will list out that the image if the picture is of a car.

Think about how difficult this would be if you skipped out on trying to use machine learning or with the neural networks and instead tried to use some of the forms of conventional coding to get it all done. It may be possible to code with Python to do this, but it is really difficult. But with the neural network, that can be done with the help of a special Python library, this system becomes so much better to work with.

For the algorithm to work, you would need to provide the system with an image of the car. The neural network would then be able to look over the picture. It would start with the first layer, which would be the outside edges of the car. Then it would go through a number of other layers that help the neural network understand if there were any unique characteristics that are present in the picture that outlines that it is a car. If the program is good at doing the job, it is going to get better at finding some of the smallest details of the car, including things like its windows and even wheel patterns.

There could potentially be a lot of different layers that come with this one, but the more layers and details that the neural network can find the more accurately it will be able to predict what kind of car is in front of it. If your neural network is accurate in identifying the car model, it is going to learn from this lesson. It will remember some of these patterns and characteristics that showed up in the car model and will store them for use later. The next time that they encounter the same kind of car model, they will be able to make a prediction pretty quickly.

When we bring out one of the neural networks, you will have to choose one, and then stick with it when you are looking through a huge amount of pictures that are out there, and then decide on one that has some defining features inside of it all. For example, this is something that is pretty popular to work with when it comes to software that is able to recognize facial features of someone else to determine if they should be in one place or not.

All of the information that you need to use for the facial recognition program is not going to be available to you ahead of time with this method. But you still have a lot of power here because you can use the neural network to help teach the computer how it is supposed to recognize the right faces, even if you don't have all of the right information ahead of time. It is also a good method to work with, and really effective when you would like to work with some recognition software that can help us look at different animals, one that can define the car models, and so much more.

As you can imagine here, there are going to be a ton of advantages that show up using this neural network idea for machine learning. One of these advantages is that you cause this method without having to be in control of the statistics of your algorithm. Even if you aren't in control of the statistics or have them all present right now, or even you aren't sure how to use them, you will find that the neural network can be used to handle all of the complex relationships that can show up through this process. This is going to be true between both the independent and dependent variables, even if you have some nonlinear variables.

Of course, there are some disadvantages that can show up with using the neural network, which means that you may not use it all of the time. You may find that one of the biggest challenges is the cost of computing is going to be a bit higher than what some companies want to work with. Sometimes, even with all of the great things that the neural network can help with, the cost is going to be too much, and it won't be worth it. But for those who want to work on some of the more advanced processes that are out there, this can be a great algorithm to use with machine learning that can really help you to get started.

Chapter 8: Working with K-Means Clustering

Another important algorithm that we can spend some time on when working in machine learning is known as the k-means clustering. This is an idea that is pretty basic to work with, especially in terms of the other things that we can do with machine learning, but it is going to help us to see a lot of results in a quick and effective way compared to some of the other algorithms that we want to use. The basic idea that we can remember when working with this algorithm is that we want to take in all of the data we want to use, data that hasn't been labeled, and then we put it together into some clusters based on where each data point has fallen.

Clustering is a great option to use, and it gives us a good example of working with unsupervised machine learning. This method is going to be applied any time the data you want to use isn't labeled ahead of time for you. The goal of using this in machine learning is to make it easier for someone to identify the clusters or the groups that are found inside a set of data.

The main purpose of working with these clusters is that the objects that fall into one cluster will be related in a close manner to all of the other points that fall in there as well. And then all of the objects that are in one cluster are not going to have much, if anything, in common with the objects in another cluster. This is an important metric to look out for because it shows us how strong the relationship is between two or more objects in your set of data.

This idea of clustering, especially with the K-means clustering method is going to be used often in the process of data mining, and this is even truer if the data mining is exploratory. It could also have some use with other fields, including computer graphics, data compression machine learning, bioinformatics, image analysis, pattern recognition and information retrieval to name a few options.

The algorithm is then going to get to work by forming some clusters with the data, based on how similar the values of the data are. At this point, the programmer needs to come in and specify what they would like the value of K to be, keeping in mind that K is going to be the number of clusters that you expect the algorithm to make out of that data. You can choose how many clusters you would like to work with based on the kind of data you are working with and what kind of information or insights you are hoping to get out of that data as well.

At this point, we are going to see that the K-means clustering, after you have presented the data and decided on how many values of K you were going to work with, will go through three steps in a way that is more iterative. The three steps that happen here will include:

1. You will want to start with the Euclidian distance between each data instance and the centroids for all of the clusters.
2. Assign the instances of data to the cluster of centroids with the nearest distance possible.
3. Calculate the new centroid values, depending on the mean values of the coordinates of the data instances from the corresponding cluster.

How to Work with This Algorithm

For us to get started with this, we need to know that the input that we put in for K is going to be found in the matrix of X, for the most part and you will be able to add in a bit of organization to your choice here to ensure that the rows you create will be with a different sample. And then the columns that you create are going to include a different kind of factor or feature as well. To ensure that this happens the way that you want, it is important to follow the right steps for this algorithm, and those are:

Start out by choosing the centers that should show up for the clusters you are choosing. If you are not positive about where the centers should be to get the best results, it is then time for you to start out with a random point in the information and use that for the center in the beginning. If you mess around with the clusters a bit later and find that you want to move the center around, then this is a possibility as well.

The second step that we need to focus on here is to create the main loop. After you have taken some time to experiment with where the centers of your clusters will be, it is time to decide which cluster you are going to use for each of the points in your set of data. You can take a look at the samples that are provided and then choose the center of the cluster that it fits in with the best.

For the third step, it is time to do a few re-calculations of the centers of your clusters. When we are doing this, the new centers are going to be based on the center points that you already assigned to each part. This makes it a bit easier to work with because when it is all said and done, you can take all of those samples and figure out the means between all of the centers. And once you have that answer, this provides you with the k-means.

This is a step that we will do a few times, and that we continue with until the algorithm comes to convergence. This means that there are no more changes that we can make to the centers of the clusters, or to the assignments that we are working with. For most of the sets of data that you do, this can be limited down in just five steps at most although a few times it will take more.

As you work through this one, you should notice that it is going to be quite a bit different than what we see with the gradient descent used with another form of deep learning. With these gradient descents, we end up with a lot of iterations before there is a convergence, and with this algorithm, it only takes a few steps to get it all done.

To help us get a better idea of what is going on with this algorithm and what we are seeing, let's take a look at how all of this works, and how we come up with our own k-means in the process:

```
--- - ^-
| 1 |  | 2 |
---   ---

| |
| |
| |
- * - ---
| 3 |  | 4 |
---   ---
```

This is going to be our initialization point. Here we will have four vectors that are going to be labeled as 1, 2, 3, and 4. The two cluster centers, which are k=2, have been randomly assigned in this one to points 2 and 3.

We used the (*) and the (^) signs to help denote these. It is now time, to begin with, the main loop.

The first step that we need to do is decide which cluster each of our points are going to belong to. We are going to see that the points 1 and 3 are going to be the cluster center on the left because they are both closer to that one than the center cluster. And then the points 2 and 4 will be in the center cluster on the right because they fit closer to that one.

The second step is to do a recalculation of the cluster centers based on the points that will belong to that cluster. The (*) cluster is going to move in between 1 and 3 because this ends up being the main of those two points. The same thing is going to happen with the (^) cluster but it will move between 2 and 4 since this will be the mean of these 2 points. It is pretty easy to come up with the mean for these two points because of the lower amount of data points, but with more complex data, you would be able to use an algorithm to make it happen. For this example, you would need to use the following code:

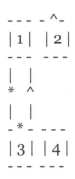

```
 _ _ _  _  ^ _
| 1 |   | 2 |
 _ _ _   _ _ _
|   |   |   |
*       ^
|   |   |
 _ * _   _ _ _
| 3 |   | 4 |
 _ _ _   _ _ _
```

You will not see any changes happen in the subsequent iterations so for this example, we are going to be all done.

Adding the Soft K-Means to Your Code

Above we took a look at some of the coding that we can work with on this algorithm, but there are definitely more steps that we are able to take a look at here. But with this in mind, we are going to implement a few of the different ideas that we have brought to the table here, and use Python and other parts of machine learning to create a model that works with the K-Means algorithm. The process that we will use here though is to find a way to implement the soft K-Means into the code we are writing.

The best method that we can use to make this happen is to make sure that we get started on some standard imports, and then have them work with what is known as the utility function. This is going to be pretty similar to what we would do with the Euclidean distance, and the cost function can come in together with this. The formula that you will be able to use to ensure that this all happens will include:

```
import numpy as np
import matplotlib.pyplot as plt


def d(u, v):
    diff = u - v
    return diff.dot(diff)


def cost(X, R, M):
    cost = 0
    for k in xrange(len(M)):
        for n in xrange(len(X)):
            cost += R[n,k]*d(M[k], X[n])
    return cost
```

After we have time to write out this code, we will need to spend some time defining the function that we want to use. The purpose of the function here is that it can help us to run the algorithm for k-means before we plot out the results. This is going to provide us with a nice scatterplot where the color is going to represent how much of the set of data will fall into each of the clusters that we provide. The code that we need to use make sure all of this happens will include:

```
def plot_k_means(X, K, max_iter=20, beta=1.0):
    N, D = X.shape
    M = np.zeros((K, D))
    R = np.ones((N, K)) / K

    # initialize M to random
    for k in xrange(K):
        M[k] = X[np.random.choice(N)]

    grid_width = 5
    grid_height = max_iter / grid_width
    random_colors = np.random.random((K, 3))
    plt.figure()

    costs = np.zeros(max_iter)
    for i in xrange(max_iter):
        # moved the plot inside the for loop
        colors = R.dot(random_colors)
        plt.subplot(grid_width, grid_height, i+1)
        plt.scatter(X[:,0], X[:,1], c=colors)

        # step 1: determine assignments / resposibilities
        # is this inefficient?
        for k in xrange(K):
            for n in xrange(N):
                R[n,k] = np.exp(-beta*d(M[k], X[n])) / np.sum(
np.exp(-beta*d(M[j], X[n])) for j in xrange(K) )

        # step 2: recalculate means
        for k in xrange(K):
            M[k] = R[:,k].dot(X) / R[:,k].sum()

        costs[i] = cost(X, R, M)
```

```
if i > 0:
    if np.abs(costs[i] - costs[i-1]) < 10e-5:
        break

plt.show()
```

As you go through and write out the code above, there is something that we need to notice before we continue. We can see here that both the R and the M above will turn into matrices. The R is going to turn into a matrix because it is able to hold onto the 2 indices, the n, and the k. Then we see M turn into a matrix because it will contain what is known as the K individual D-dimensional vector.

The variable that is considered the beta here is going to control how to spread out or even how fuzzy, the memberships are in the cluster, and we are going to call these the hyperparameter. At this point, we can then go through the code and create our own main function, one that is able to create random clusters and then call up the functions that we defined above. The code that we can use to make this happen will include:

```
def main():
    # assume 3 means
    D = 2 # so we can visualize it more easily
    s = 4 # separation so we can control how far apart the means
are
```

```python
mu1 = np.array([0, 0])
mu2 = np.array([s, s])
mu3 = np.array([0, s])

N = 900 # number of samples
X = np.zeros((N, D))
X[:300, :] = np.random.randn(300, D) + mu1
X[300:600, :] = np.random.randn(300, D) + mu2
X[600:, :] = np.random.randn(300, D) + mu3

# what does it look like without clustering?
plt.scatter(X[:,0], X[:,1])
plt.show()

K = 3 # luckily, we already know this
plot_k_means(X, K)

# K = 5 # what happens if we choose a "bad" K?
# plot_k_means(X, K, max_iter=30)

# K = 5 # what happens if we change beta?
# plot_k_means(X, K, max_iter=30, beta=0.3)


if __name__ == '__main__':
    main()
```

At this point, we have been able to talk about the K-Means clustering algorithm and even looked at an example of the code that you can write with this machine learning algorithm. Take some time to look at this code, and even type it into your Python compiler to see what we can do to make it perform in the process.

Chapter 9: The K-Nearest Neighbors Algorithm with Python

The next algorithm that we are going to take a look at is the K-Nearest Neighbors or KNN. This is going to be a good example that comes with supervised machine learning so we will be able to take a closer look at how this kind of algorithm. When you bring out the KNN algorithm you will have the goal of searching through your data to find the k most similar examples of your chosen instance that you are trying to work with. Once we are able to do this and see even a little success then this algorithm is able to look through the information that is there and summarize it in a manner that you can understand. At the end of all this, the algorithm will then be able to use the results out of this to provide you with predictions.

Any time that you decide to work with this kind of model, you will work with a kind of learning that is set up to be pretty competitive with the different points. This is important because it is going to make sure that all of the parts that are present will compete with one another in the model. This is a great thing for you because it will provide us with the best predictions based on the information that you provide to the algorithm.

The KNN algorithm is nice because it helps us to work on a few tasks that we may not see with some of the other algorithms that we can look over in the next few chapters. For example, in some cases, it can be seen as an approach that is a bit lazier to work with mainly because it is not meant to create any of the models that we need here, at least not ahead of time. You have to go in and ask for it to make a brand-new prediction. Depending on the situation we want to use the algorithm for, the prediction will make sure that the data we are working with is a new and current as possible each time, and then will kick out a new prediction when you need to.

There are other possible algorithms that we can use that will provide us with a good prediction on a regular basis, and sometimes just when you put in new data. There are going to be times when this process is going to be helpful. But if you want to see what happens with just specific types of data, and at the times that work the best for you then it is best to work with the KNN algorithm to get it done, rather than just using all of the information that you can find, and this data can be extensive.

There are a ton of benefits that a programmer is going to receive when they decide to work with this particular algorithm. When you are working with the KNN algorithm, you are better able to cut through some of the noise that is present in the set of data. We have to be careful with some of the noise that is there because sometimes it is really loud, especially with more data that you collect, and cutting out some of the noise is going to help us to make sure we get the relevant and helpful information, rather than a bunch of stuff that we can't use.

Unlike some of the other algorithms that we can work with, the KNN algorithm is going to appear to take on more data than some of the other algorithms that can limit their information and data. This means that the KNN algorithm will be able to handle any set of data that you want to work with, whether it is a large set of data or a small set of data.

One of the disadvantages that we can see with working on this algorithm is that often the costs of computation are going to be higher. This is going to be even truer when we are looking at it compared to some of the other similar algorithms out there. The reason that we see these costs as so high is that this algorithm is going to look at all of the data points, rather than clustering method, and then sends out the prediction. Looking at all of the data points makes the work that much harder.

When Should I Use the KNN Algorithm?

The first question that many programmers are going to have concerning this algorithm is when they should decide to work with it. The KNN algorithm works the best on both classification and regression problems, as long as they are going to work on predictions. With that in mind, you will find that this algorithm is going to be used the most with classification problems. We can also look at the three most important things that you should consider when evaluating the KNN technique and deciding whether or not to use it, and these will include:

1. Take a look at the output you will receive and determine how easy it will be to interpret.

2. The calculation of how long this algorithm will take and if you really have that much time to spare.
3. The predictive power of the model.

When you compare this algorithm side by side with a few other algorithms including options like the logistic regression and random forests, you may see that it will do well across the most common parameters and other considerations. The reason that data science and machine learning programmers are going to work with this algorithm is that the results it provides are easy to read through and the calculations that you get will be lower.

A Look at How the KNN Algorithm Works

As we will see, there are a number of different algorithms that fit into machine learning, and each of them works slightly differently. This is a great thing to know about because it ensures that we are going to find the method we want to use in our coding, and we will get the results in no time. With this in mind, there are a few steps that you can follow when it comes to working on the KNN algorithm, and these include:

1. Load the data into the algorithm for it to read through.
2. Initialize the value that you are going to use and rely on for k.
3. When you are ready to get the predicted class, iteration from one to the total number of the data points that you use for training, you can use the following steps to help.

   a. Start by calculating the distance that is in between each of your test data, and each row of your training data. We are going to work with the Euclidean distance as our metric for distance since it's the most popular method. Some of the other metrics that you may choose to work with here include the cosine and Chebyshev.
   b. Sort the calculated distances going in ascending order based on their distance values.
   c. Get the k rows from the sorted array.
   d. Get the most frequent class for these rows.
   e. Return back the class prediction.

Finding the Best K Value

The final thing that we will take a look at here is the idea of finding the best k value to work with. This chapter has taken a look at how this algorithm works, but we have not had time to really look at how you can pick the most optimal value of K to work with. The best method you can use though is to work with cross-validation.

We have to remember here is that you can use cross-validation to help us figure out an estimate of the validation error. To help us accomplish this task though, we need to hold out on a subset of the training set and use it later, rather than adding it to the process of building a model.

We can look at an example of how this will work, saying that our example has a validation that is 10-fold. With that in mind, cross-validation is going to involve the programming going through and randomly dividing up the set they use for training into ten separate groups, which will be known as the folds. You want to keep these as even in size as you can. From that, 90 percent of the data is what you will use to train the model you are creating. Then with the other ten percent, it will be used to help test, or validate, this model and make sure that it has learned what you expected in the process.

It is always a good idea to go through and not just do a training set on the model you work with, but also a testing set. This testing set will make sure that the algorithm is actually learning what you want. If things are not looking good and the accuracy levels are not where you think they should be, then this is a sign that something is off with your training sets, such as the data you use for training is inaccurate or not high quality.

Chapter 10: The Support Vector Machines

The next algorithm that we can include on our list is known as the support vector machine or SVM. This SVM is going to be something that can be useful to many programmers, whether they focus on machine learning or data science because it helps with many of the challenges that come up with both classification and regression problems. With this algorithm, a lot of the work that has to be done on the problems of classification can add a level of trickiness to some of the work that you are doing, and with some of the other methods and algorithms that are present, it may seem impossible to get things fixed. The good news here is that the algorithm for SVM is going to ensure that you can tackle the challenge and get you some great results in no time.

If you decide that you want to make a model that relies on the SVM algorithm, you will need to take each of the items that are in your data set and then find a way to plot them so that they show up in just one point on an n-dimensional space. The N is going to be the number of features that you would like to plan to use with this. Then you can take the value that you come up with here from those features and then find a way to translate it over to the value that will show up on your coordinates.

The job that we need to work on once we have been able to reach this point will include determining where our hyperplane needs to fall. The reason we need to spend some time on this hyperplane is that this is the part that is going to make it easier to see what differences are present in the various classes that we work with.

You may notice at this point that the SVM algorithm may present you with not just one, but multiple support vectors that you need to work with. The good news is that many of the ones that you see here are simply the coordinates of any individual observations that show up. Sometimes though, we need to make some decisions on which one we want to look at and we want to base our model and information on. The SVM can help us separate out the information that we have into some classes, and there are going to be two main ones that you want to put all of your focus on including the hyperplane and the line.

To this point, a lot of what we are discussing in this chapter is going to seem confusing and it may not make a lot of sense. The SVM algorithm is going to be something that a lot of programmers may skip out on because they worry that it is not going to be worth the hassle that we put into it. But with all of the benefits that happen with this particular algorithm, it is worth our time to learn what this is all about.

To help us learn more about the SVM algorithm, we can look at some of the best steps that a programmer is able to take to sort through the data and pass it through the SVM algorithm. First, we need to be able to look at the hyperplane that we can work with. As you go through here though, we may find more than one hyperplane that you can choose from. This can turn into another challenge to work with because you have options, and you want to make sure that with all of those options, you end up with the one that will give you the best predictions and options out of that data.

The best thing to realize here though is that even with more than one hyperplane to work with, there are a few steps that are pretty easy that we are able to work with to ensure that you don't base all of your information and insights on the wrong plan. These steps are going to include:

- We are going to start out with three hyperplanes that we will call 1, 2, and 3. Then we are going to spend time figuring out which hyperplane is right so that we can classify the star and the circle.
- The good news is there is a pretty simple rule that you can follow so that it becomes easier to identify which hyperplane is the right one. The hyperplane that you want to go with will be the one that segregates your classes the best.
- That one was easy to work with, but in the next one, our hyperplanes of 1, 2, and 3 are all going through the classes and they segregate them in a manner that is similar. For example, all of the lines or these hyperplanes are going to run parallel with each other. From here you may find that it is hard to pick which hyperplane is the right one.
- For the issue that is above, we will need to use what is known as the margin. This is basically the distance that occurs between the hyperplane and the nearest data point from either of the two classes. Then you will be able to get some numbers that can help you out. These numbers

may be closer together, but they will point out which hyperplane is going to be the best.

Now, when we go back and look at the example that was talked about above in the example that we have, you will find that this SVM is a really useful and helpful tool when it comes to machine learning. Any time that you search through some of the data points that you want to work with, and you see that there is a steady or a large margin that points out a type of separation, then this algorithm is going to be the one you want to rely on to get all of the work done.

In addition, the amount of effectiveness that comes out of this model or this algorithm is going to see an increase any time that you work with a project that has a dimensional space higher than what is seen as normal. You may not use this model or this algorithm as often as some of the others, but even so, working with this particular technique is still useful because it will help you to use a subset of the training points that come with the function for the decision, which is the support vector, and when the memory of the program you are working on is high enough to allow us to do this.

The SVM algorithm can provide us with a lot of benefits when we work with machine learning and the benefits will change based on what project you plan to accomplish here. There are times when it may not be the best option or model to work with. For example, if you have a set of data that is pretty large, then this model doesn't work as well because the results that it provides to us are usually not that accurate. The training time with the larger data set is going to be high, and this can be a disappointment if you would like to make sure you can read through the information and get an insight or prediction in a short amount of time. And if you end up with a few target classes that have some overlap, the SVM is going to behave differently than you would expect, and you need to be on the lookout for all of that.

Chapter 11: Other Options of Machine Learning with the Help of Python

To add on a few of the topics that we have talked about previously, and the other algorithms that come with machine learning, there are going to be quite a few other options that are available for all of your machine learning needs. These can be valuable for us to learn about depending on the projects that we are trying to create, or what kind of information you are looking to gain out of all that data you collected and are sorting through. This chapter will take a look at a few of the other machine learning algorithms available for you to complete your model and get things done

Naïve Bayes

The first option that we can take a look at is going to be the Naïve Bayes algorithm. To help us understand the way that this algorithm works, we need to bring out our imagination a bit. To do this, let's imagine that we are working on a classification problem for our project, but our goal is to also come up with a good hypothesis, one that is actually going to work. And we also want to work with some design that is going to allow you to have a new feature and discussion based on the amount of importance that comes with each variable has.

While this may seem like it is going to take a lot of work to accomplish, and like we are trying to stuff a ton of things into a short amount of time, it is something that has to be done. Once you have taken the time that is needed to collect all of that information, it is likely that you will have a few of the key stakeholders in the company who will show a bit of interest in what you are doing, and what model you are trying to produce with it. Often these individuals are going to want to see this model long before all of the work is done.

This often presents a kind of dilemma for a lot of data scientists because they aren't sure how to show all of the unfinished models in a way that others are going to be to explain in the process. The data scientist is going to want to present information that makes sense to their stakeholders, but the work is not going to be done all of the time and this is why it is often hard to accomplish.

In many of the situations where you are going to sort through and work with your data, you may end up with thousands of points of data and often more, that you want to have shown up on the model. There can even be some of the newer variables that show up in this and can make things difficult to show things during the testing and training phase. The data scientist has to figure out how to make all of this happen.

The good thing to remember here is that there is an algorithm option that is presented to make it easier. It is meant to help you through some of the earlier stages of your work, and still show what you plan to do with some of that data later on. This algorithm is known as the Naïve Bayes algorithm and it is a great way for the data scientist to work with a few demonstrations to showcase your model, no matter how early you are in the development stage.

As we work more with this kind of algorithm, we will find that there are a lot of benefits of working with it, and this is why many programmers want to work with it in the first place. This model is an easy one to use, especially for those who are just starting out with deep learning and machine learning. You will find that it is also really effective when we need to make a few predictions for our set of data and which classes they will end up in.

This also makes it easier because we are able to keep things as simple as possible during this process. Even though the Naïve Bayes algorithm is going to be simple, it does perform really well. In fact even when we have time to compare it with some of the algorithms that are seen as a higher class, and some of the more sophisticated options, this one is able to perform really well in the process.

Even though we can find a ton of benefits that come with using the Naïve Bayes algorithm, there are negatives that we need to focus on as well. The first thing that we need to be aware of is that if you want to set it with some categorical variables, you need to make sure that any of the data you plan to test out has not already gone through a set of data for training in the past. You may find that this particular algorithm is also going to run into problems when it comes to making predictions that are accurate, and often the sets of data that are going to be assigned to your information will be based on probability more than you want.

The Regression Algorithm

The next algorithm that you can consider is known as the regression analysis. This is the type that you will want to look into when you want to see if there is a relationship, and what type of relationship, that is able to show up between the dependent variables and the predictor variables. You will see that this technique is going to work well when you are looking to check out whether there is a causal relationship between the forecasting, the variable you are working with, or the time-series modeling in place. The point of the regression algorithm in machine learning is that it is going to help take all of your information and fit it onto a line, or a simple curve, as much as you can. This may not always happen depending on the data points that you are working with, but it can work well to help you see if there are any kinds of factors in common with the data points that will be seen on a graph.

There are many companies that will use the regression algorithm in order to help them make great predictions that will increase their profits. You will be able to use it in order to come up with a great estimation of the sales growth for the company while still basing it on how the economic conditions in the market are doing right at this moment.

The great thing about this is that you are able to add in any information that you would like to use. You can add information about the past and the current economy to this particular algorithm, such as your past and current economic information, and then this gives you an idea of how the growth is going to go in the future. Of course, you do need to have the right information about the company to make this happen.

An example of this is when we use the regression algorithm, and find that the company is already growing at the same rate as what other industries are doing in the economy. You a then use this kind of information to help you make some predictions based on that information and can plan out how you will run your business in the future.

There are a few variations that come with using the regression algorithm and you have to go with the one that makes the best sense based on your model and what you are trying to do. Some of the most common regression algorithms that you use with machine learning will include the linear regression, the stepwise regression, the ridge regression, the polynomial regression, and the logistic regression.

As you can see, when you decide to pull out the regression algorithms you will find that there are a number of benefits that you will see as well. The first benefit here is that you are going to be using these algorithms to make it easy for anyone using the information to see whether or not there is a relationship of some kind between the variables that are independent and the variables that are dependent. The regression algorithm is going to show you the impact that will happen any time that a new variable is added to the mix and whether this will be a positive or a negative thing.

We also have to take a look at some of the disadvantages that can come with the regression algorithm. The biggest challenge that comes with the regression algorithm is that you will notice it is not going to work well with those classification problems. The regression algorithm and the classification problems are not going to fit well together because the constraints between both are going to be very different from one another, and you will find that trying to get the two types of problems and solutions becomes tedious.

Working with the Clustering Algorithms

While we did take a look at one of the clustering options for algorithms earlier, but we are going to look a bit more closely with this here and see some of the basics, and the benefits, that come with these clustering algorithms. The different clustering algorithms are going to fit into the category of unsupervised machine learning, so you can set them up to learn on their own and the whole program is going to learn on its own as well.

When we decide to work with some of the options for clustering algorithms, we have to remember that keeping things simple is important. This method is going to take some of the data you have been able to collect, and then it will make clusters are going to come with it. Before you start up with this model, you will get to have in the model and how you want the information to fit into it. This is going to depend on how much data you are working with, and what information you hope to get from all of this process

Let's say that you are doing a process where you want all of the information sorted between two categories, maybe splitting up between the male and the female customers to see how each group acts in your store. But if you are working on a problem where you want to set up the age groups of your customers to see if you are reaching the right target audience, then maybe you will have four or more clusters. You can decide this based on the information that you have on hand.

With the clustering algorithm, you will be able to have the input of the number of clusters that you would like to work with, and then the program is able to take all of the points of data and divide them into each cluster. These clusters are going to be divided up based on which features they match with the best.

One thing that you will notice with this algorithm that is nice is that it is going to be able to handle a lot of, if not most of, the work that you want to do. This is because it is going to be in charge of how many data points will be fitting into each of the clusters that you decide to work with. To keep everything in line and organized, we will call all of those main clusters that we created the cluster centroids.

So, when we are looking at these clusters and we notice that one of them tends to have a lot of points that fall inside of it, you can safely and easily make some assumption that all of these data points will have something in common with one another, or they are similar in some big manner. This is how they all ended up in the same cluster in the first place.

Once you have seen the program create all of these clusters and the original ones are formed, we can then take each of the individual ones and divide them up to end up with some more sets of clusters if we want to see what is in the data even more. Sometimes, based on what you are hoping to find in the process, you will go through this several times until you can learn everything that is necessary out of the data you collect. The goal here is that we want to go through this process enough times that we end up with some centroids that do not change from one iteration to another.

There are a few benefits and reasons why we would work with these clustering algorithms to make sure the program is doing some machine learning and acting in the manner that we want. First doing our computations with the help of a clustering algorithm is actually going to be easy and pretty efficient when it comes to costs, especially when we compare it over to other methods, such as supervised machine learning. If you would like to do a classification problem, then the clustering algorithm will be one of the best and most efficient to get it all done.

There are a few downsides that come with using this kind of algorithm in our work and we need to use some caution. This algorithm is not going to be able to do the kind of work that allows it to make predictions for you. If you don't categorize the centroids in the proper manner, then you may end up with a project that works with the wrong insights and a project that is done in the wrong way than what you would want.

The Markov Algorithm

The next algorithm that is on our list that we can explore a little bit is known as the Markov algorithm. This is another example that we can learn from when it comes to unsupervised machine learning. This algorithm is going to work because it takes the data that you add to it and then translates it to work with any of the other coding languages that we choose to go with. One neat feature here is that you are able to pick out the rules that you would like to use with this algorithm before you start, ensuring that the algorithm has the right parameters and will work the way that you are looking for.

Many of the programmers who work with machine learning will find that this algorithm, along with the fact that they get the freedom to set up their own rules with this, is really nice. This one also allows you to take a string of data and then see if it is working the way that you want.

Another benefit that comes with the Markov algorithm is that the programmer can work with it using several methods, rather than finding themselves stuck with just one set of rules. One of the options that you can work with here is to use the algorithm with something that is more complicated like DNA. This works by taking the sequence of DNA from one person and then use this algorithm in order to translate the information that is there into a numerical value.

The reason that we look at using this method is that it often makes things so much easier for programmers, as well as for scientists and doctors because it is easier to know what information is present when it is translated out of DNA form into words or numbers. These groups of people can then use the information to make better predictions about the future. Often the numerical data is so important to work with because it helps us understand what is being said in the data.

A good reason that a machine learning programmer is able to use the Markov algorithm is that it is a good one to use anytime that the programmers know what input they would like to use, but they may be a bit unsure about the parameters that they want to set. This algorithm is going to help us find a lot of the important and maybe hidden insights that are inside the information. In some cases, these insights are going to be hard to find without an algorithm like the Markov.

There are still going to be a few negatives aspects that come with the Markov algorithm. This algorithm, in particular, is harder to work with because you are responsible for manually going through and creating a new rule any time that you want to use it on a new programming language. For those who just plan to work with Python and none of the other coding languages, this is not such a big deal. But for those who want to use Python and a few other coding languages with the Markov algorithm, then this can become a pain.

The Q-Learning Algorithm

Now that we have some examples of supervised and unsupervised machine learning, it is time to take a look at an example of what we are able to do with a reinforcement machine learning algorithm. The first option here is going to be known as the Q-learning algorithm. With this algorithm, you will find that it ends up working the best with things like temporal difference learning. As you try to add in some of the other types of machine learning, you may notice that this is going to be one of the off-policy algorithms because it does come with the capability to learn an action-value function. What this means is that you are going to be able to see the results that you want, regardless of what state you are in at the time.

Since you are able to use this kind of machine learning algorithm no matter what function you are trying to create, it is important to start this out with some time to list any specifications that you think are needed for how the learner or the user will select their own course of action. This means you must go through a few more steps to get this to happen, but it is definitely worth your time and effort to do this.

After the programmer or the data scientist, has spent some time going through and found the action-value function that you are the most interested in using, it is then time to move on to the next step of creating the policy that is the most optimal. The best way to construct this is to use the algorithm that is present that has the highest value out of all of them. This should be chosen based on what is the highest value for your no matter what state you are choosing to work with at the time.

We can see quite a few advantages when we decide that this reinforcement machine learning algorithm is the best option for us. One of these benefits is that you will not need to take all that time or effort to put in any models of the environment for the system to compare it. You will be able to compare a few, and sometimes even quite a few, actions together, and the environment type that you are going to rely on here isn't going to be as important as it is with some of the other methods.

The SARSA Algorithm

The second option that you can work with when it comes to reinforcement machine learning is known as the SARSA algorithm. The SARSA is going to be an acronym for state action reward state action algorithm.

When you are working with this, you must take the time to describe the decision process policy that will occur in your Markov algorithm that we talked about earlier in this chapter.

This would then be the main function that you would use with the updated -value which will then rely on whatever the current state of the learner is. It can also include the reward that the learner is going to get for the selecting they make, the action that the learner chooses, and then the new state that the learner is going to be in when they are done with that action. As you can see, there are a ton of different parts that will end up coming together in order to make the SARSA work for your needs.

While there are going to be quite a few parts that need to come together to make this work, there are many programmers who believe that this is the safest algorithm to work with to help them figure out the best solution to rely on. However, there can be times when the learner is going to use a program with this algorithm, and they get a reward that is higher than what they should base on the trials that they are doing.

This is going to end up as a bigger issue with the SARSA algorithm compared to some of the others.

There are a few other issues that show up as well. For example, sometimes the learner is going to choose to go down the path that is not the most optimal at the time. Depending on how the program decides to react to all of this, it could make a difference, and bring up some issues, with how others learn and how the program will actually behave.

As we can see here, there are a lot of different types of algorithms that work well with the Python machine learning process that we have been discussing in this guidebook. These are going to come in a variety of different forms including supervised learning, unsupervised learning, and even some algorithms that fit in with the reinforcement learning as well. You can choose which one of these algorithms you would like to work with based on how you want to deal with the information and the data you have on hand.

Conclusion

Thank you for making it through to the end of *Python Machine Learning*, let's hope it was informative and able to provide you with all of the tools you need to achieve your goals.

We spent a good deal lot of time working on what machine learning is all about, and how we can work with the Python coding language in order to make all of this come together and provide us with some of the benefits that we are looking for. Many data scientists and even companies are looking more into this machine learning because there are a ton of benefits, and it helps them to finally create the models they want to search through their data, and really learn some important insights in the process.

This guidebook is the guide that you need to really make sure that you understand what machine learning is about, and how you are able to use it with the help of the Python language. We looked at some about machine learning and Python and then dived into some of the best algorithms that you can do when it is time to sort through the data you have gathered.

There are many reasons why a business will want to collect data and see what insights are inside. And working with Python machine learning will ensure that we can actually sort through the data and see some great results. When you are ready to work with Python machine learning and all that it can do for you, make sure to check out this guidebook to help you get started.

Description

You have collected all of that data, maybe from different sources, but now you are ready to dive right in and see what insights are inside. But then, you look at all of that data and realize that it would be impossible for you to ever get through it, much less in a timely manner, and you feel like you have just wasted a bunch of time in the process. Instead of giving up and going home, it is time to take a look at machine learning and what it is able to do for you.

For any business that has spent time gathering data about their industry or their company, machine learning is the logical next step. This technology is able to teach a machine or a system, teach it how to do things on its own, and then sets it loose on all of that data you have collected. If the machine learning algorithm has been set up properly, then you will be able to learn a lot of great insights and predictions and will make it easier to turn your business to the future, beating out the competition and improving the customer experience.

This guidebook is going to spend some time looking at the different aspects that we need to know about Python machine learning. This can help any business, whether big or small, who collects information and data, takes that information and uses it for your own needs. Some of the different topics that we are going to use in order to learn more about Python machine learning in this guidebook include:

- What machine learning is all about.
- The different options you can choose from with machine learning and the various algorithms to get the work done.
- The benefits that come with choosing machine learning for your business.
- A look at deep learning and how this works together with machine learning to improve your business.
- An introduction to some of the different Python libraries that work well for machine learning.
- The best machine learning algorithms that any business should know to be able to see machine learning at work, and to help them effectively sort through their data.

Machine learning with Python is one of the best ways that you can take all of that data you have collected over time and put it to good use with the best insights and predictions. When you are ready to learn more about using Python machine learning, make sure to check out this guidebook today!

www.ingramcontent.com/pod-product-compliance
Lightning Source LLC
Chambersburg PA
CBHW071142050326
40690CB00008B/1540